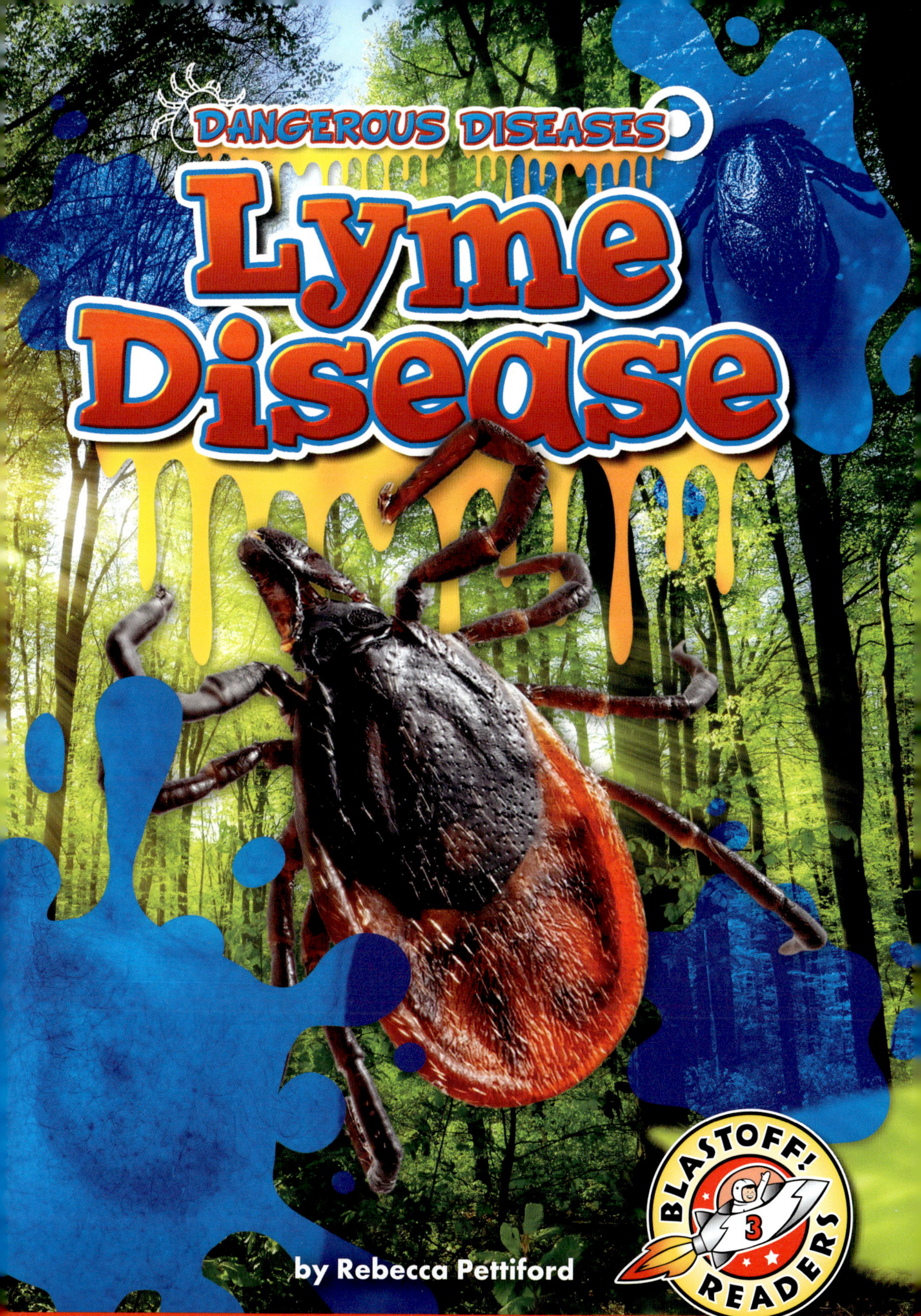

DANGEROUS DISEASES

Lyme Disease

by Rebecca Pettiford

BLASTOFF! READERS 3

BLASTOFF! READERS, AN IMPRINT OF BELLWETHER MEDIA BY FLUTTERBEE

Blastoff! Readers are carefully developed by literacy experts to build reading stamina and move students toward fluency by combining standards-based content with developmentally appropriate text.

Level 1 provides the most support through repetition of high-frequency words, light text, predictable sentence patterns, and strong visual support.

Level 2 offers early readers a bit more challenge through varied sentences, increased text load, and text-supportive special features.

Level 3 advances early-fluent readers toward fluency through increased text load, less reliance on photos, advancing concepts, longer sentences, and more complex special features.

★ **Blastoff! Universe**

This edition first published in 2027 by Bellwether Media, Inc.

For information regarding permission, write to Bellwether Media, Inc., Attention: Permissions Department, 3500 American Blvd W, Suite 150, Bloomington, MN 55431.

Library of Congress Cataloging-in-Publication Data is available at www.loc.gov or upon request from the publisher.

ISBN: 9798898800659 (hardcover)
ISBN: 9798898801892 (ebook)

Editor: Suzane Nguyen Designer: Brittany McIntosh

Printed in the United States of America, North Mankato, MN.

Table of Contents

What Is Lyme Disease?

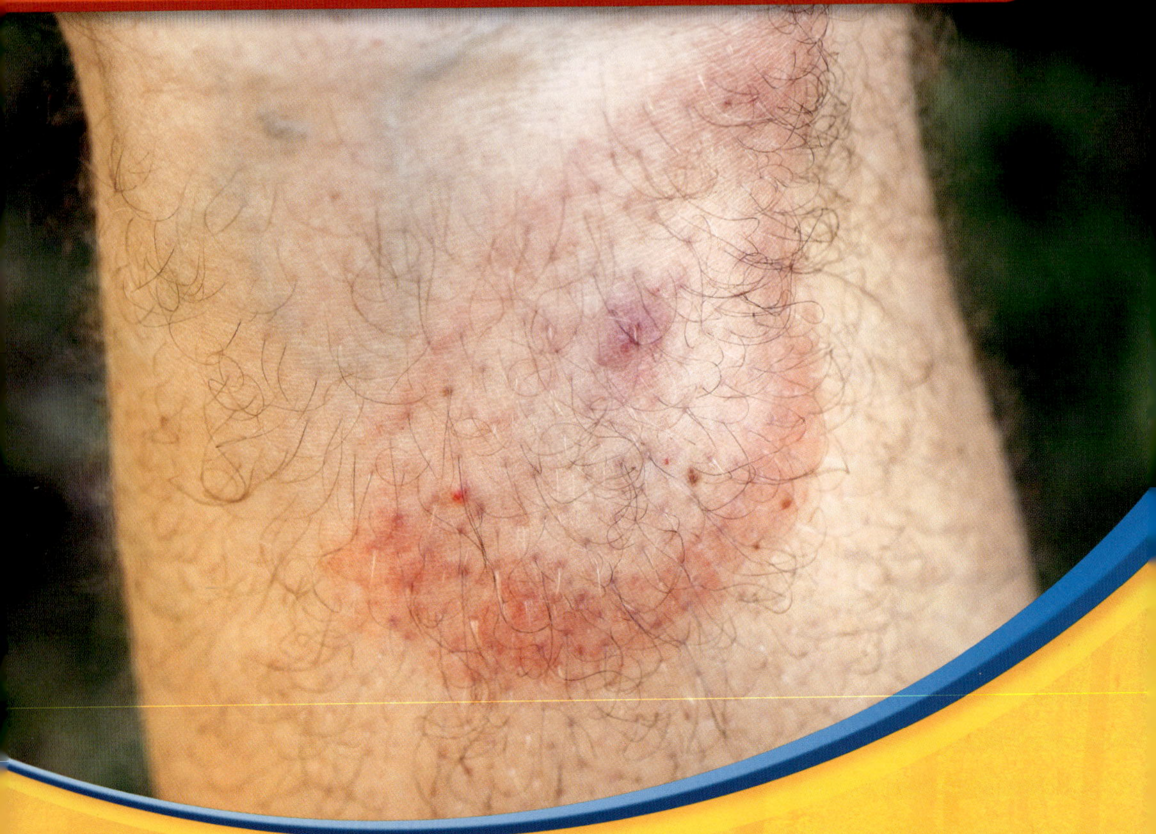

Lyme **disease** is an **infection**.
It is caused by a **bacterium**.
People get it from some **tick** bites.
Ticks get it from infected **rodents**.

Lyme disease is common in the United States.

Lyme disease has three stages. First, a bullseye-shaped **rash** appears. In the second stage, people often have pain and a **fever**.

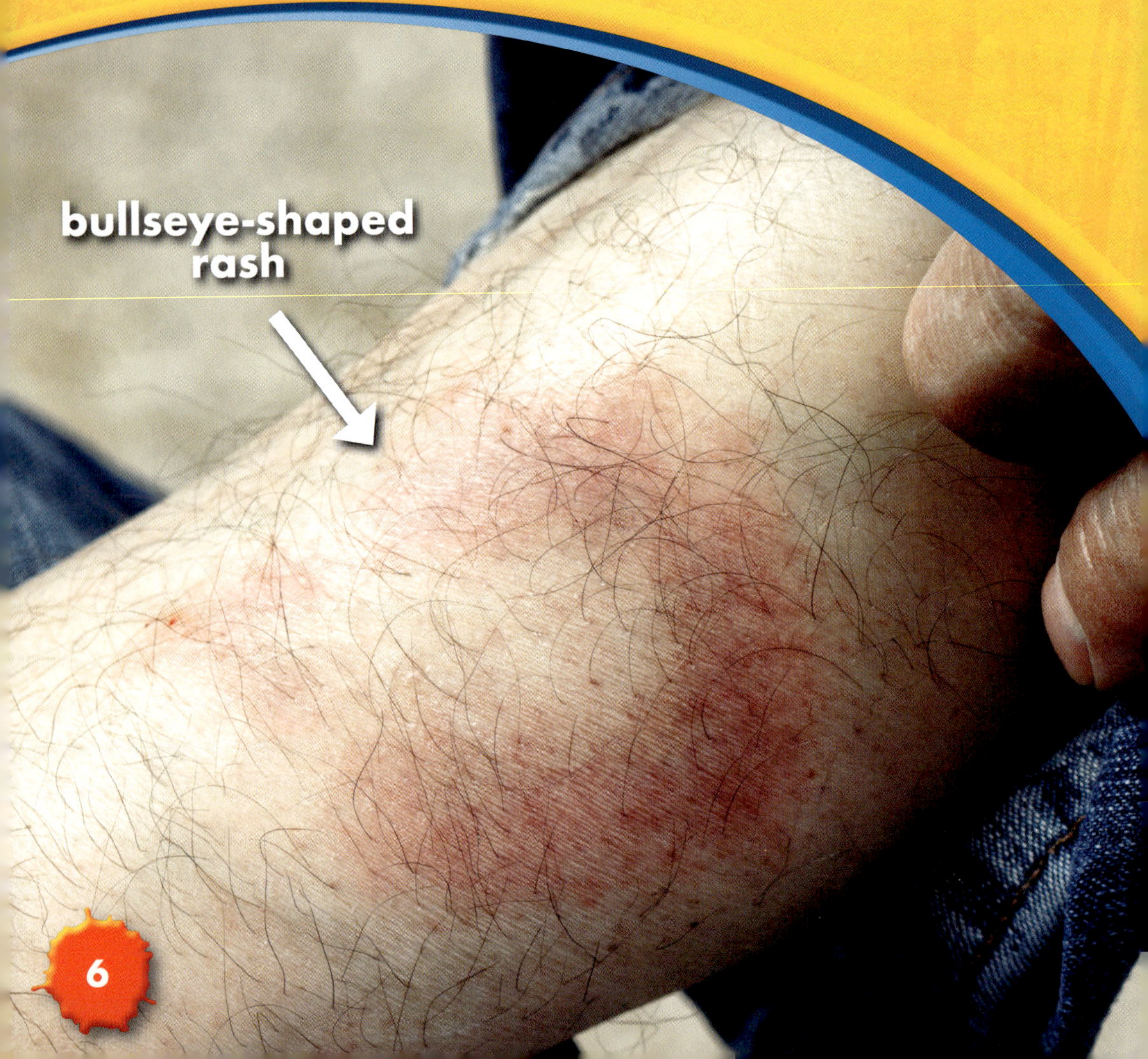

Lyme Disease in the United States

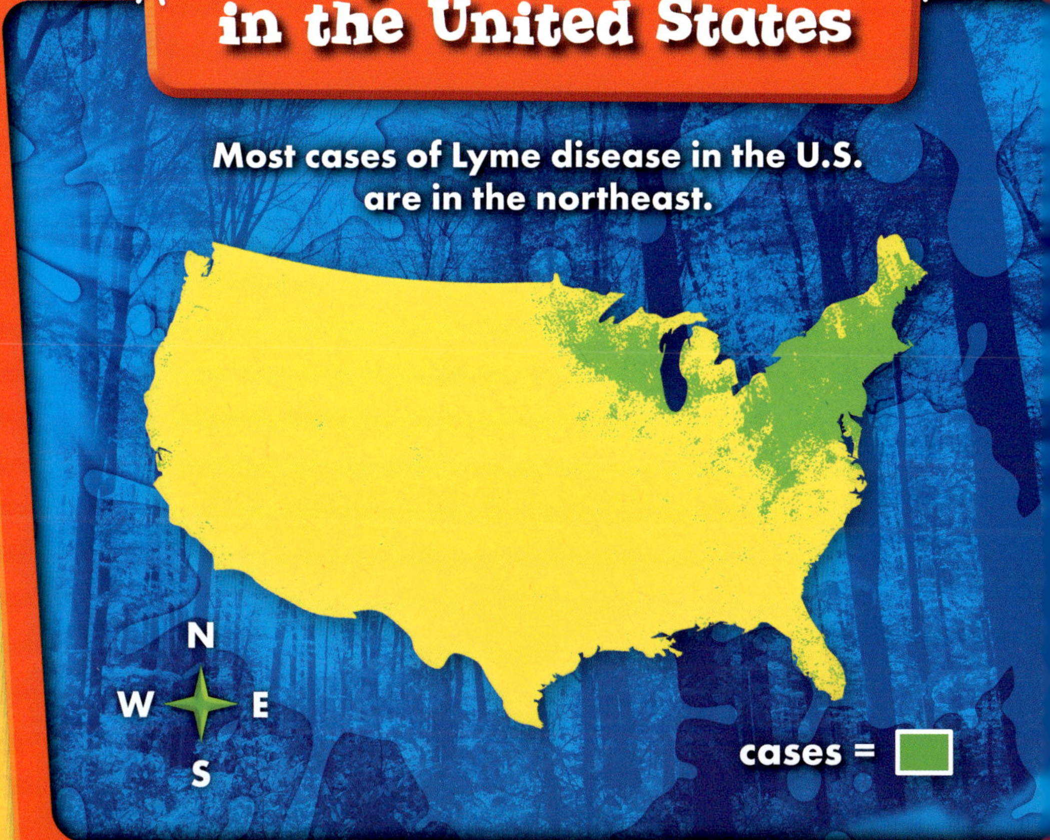

The third stage includes worse pain. Some people have trouble remembering things.

History of Lyme Disease

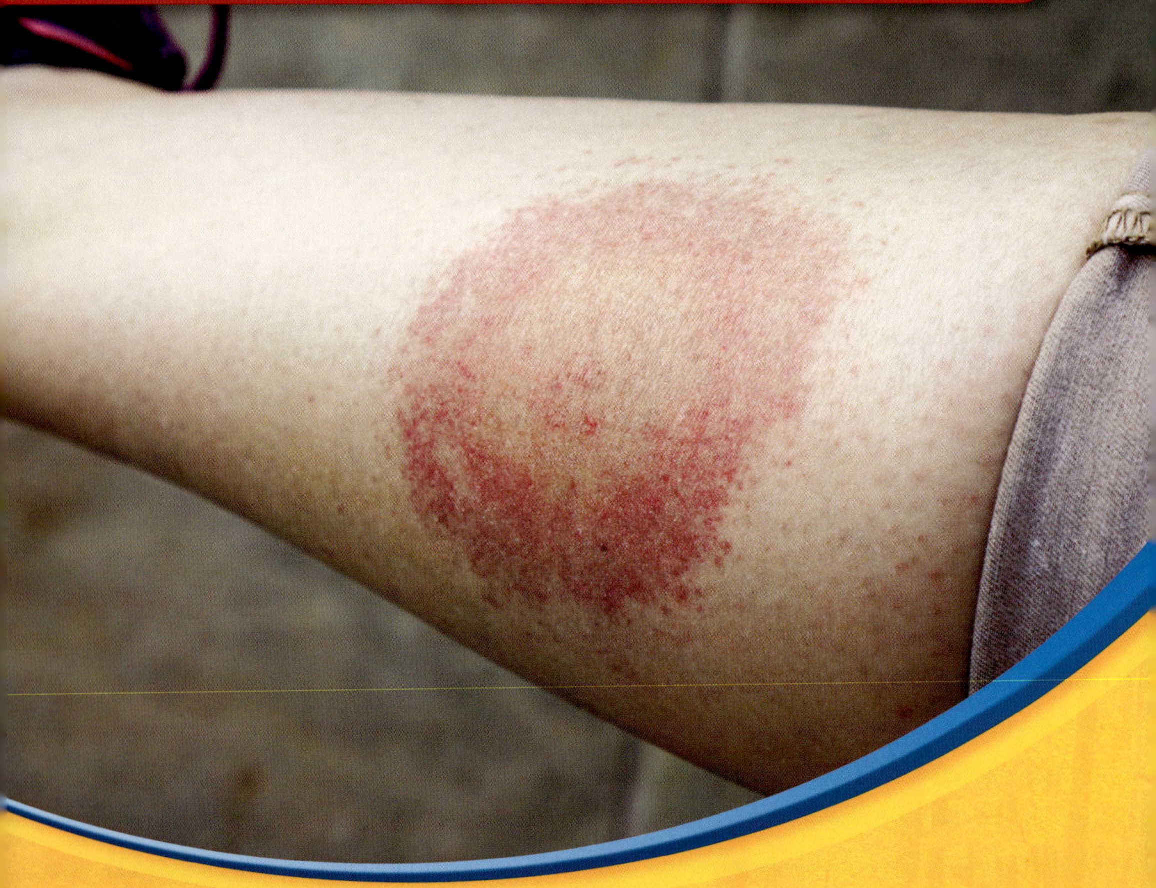

In 1883, a German doctor was the first to write about the disease.

In 1975, people in Lyme, Connecticut, were getting sick. It was the same disease the doctor had described. The disease was named after the town.

Lyme, Connecticut

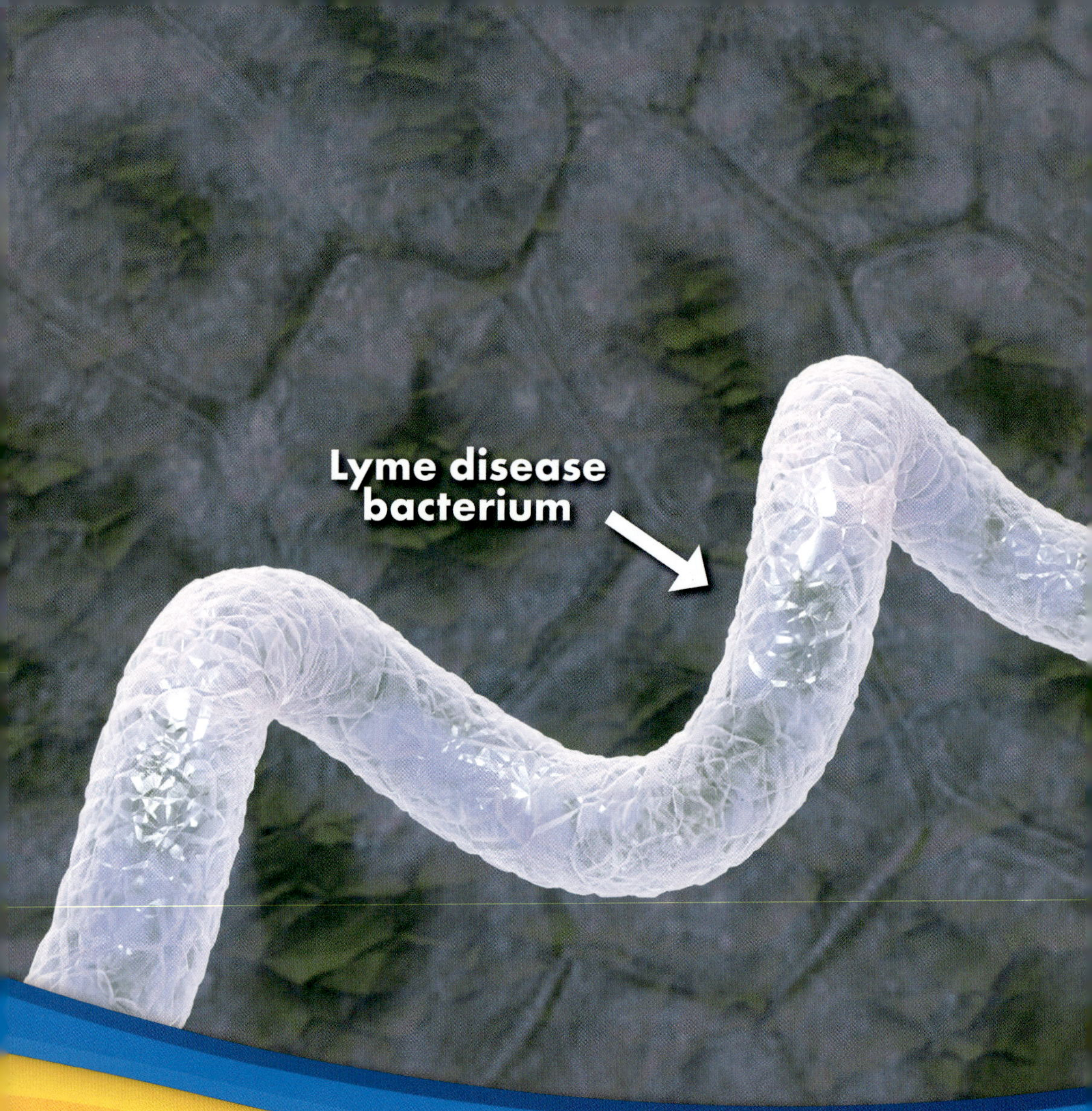

In 1982, a Swiss-American doctor found the bacterium that causes Lyme disease.

Timeline

1883
German doctor Alfred Buchwald is the first to write about the disease

1975
The first cases of the disease in the U.S. are found in Lyme, Connecticut

1982
Swiss-American doctor Willy Burgdorfer finds the bacterium that causes Lyme disease

Today, more than 450,000 people in the U.S. get Lyme disease every year.

How Does Lyme Disease Spread?

Up to half or more of all deer ticks in the U.S. carry Lyme disease. They get it when feeding on rodents with the disease.

Infected ticks spread the disease when they bite people.

The infected tick **attaches** to a person's skin. If the tick stays on for about 24 hours, the disease can spread.

The bacteria pass to a person through the tick's **saliva**.

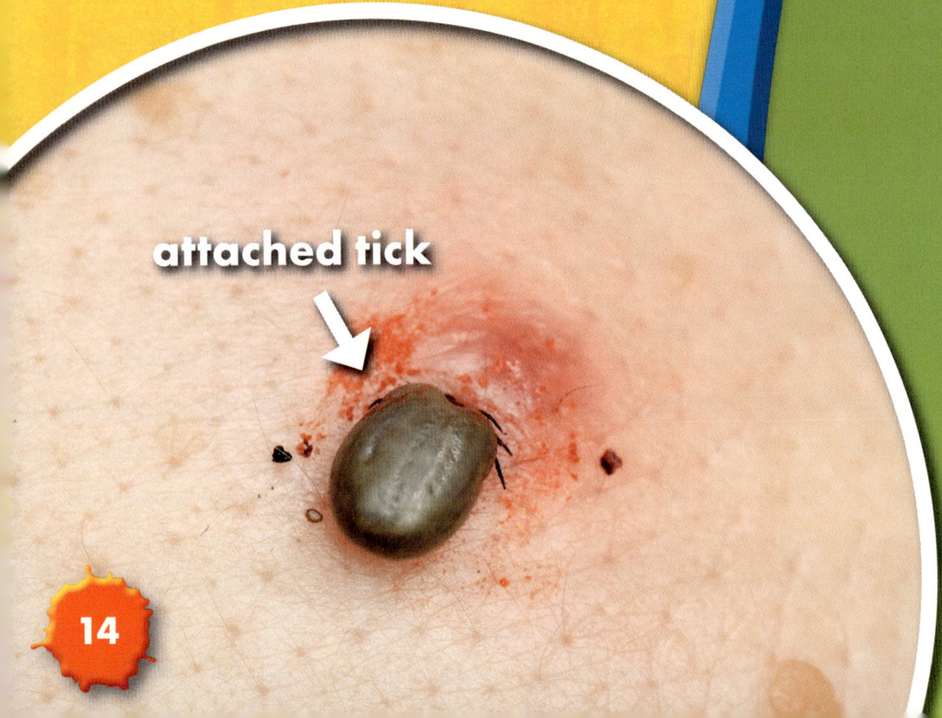

How Lyme Disease Spreads

1

A tick feeds on a rodent that carries the bacterium.

2

The infected tick bites a person.

3
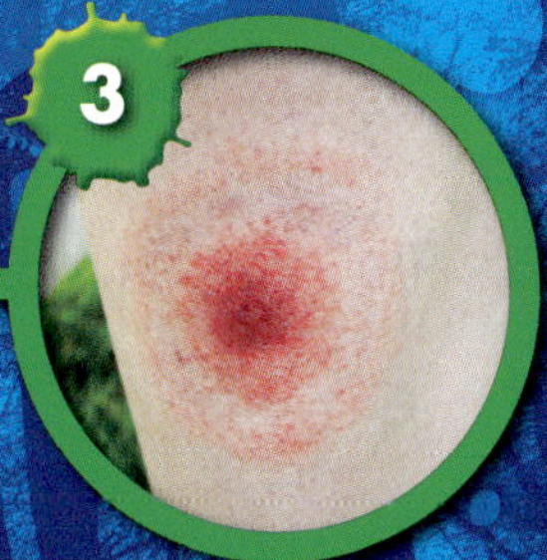

After 24 hours, an attached tick can spread Lyme disease.

Prevention and Treatment

Ticks like the woods and tall grass. Wear long sleeves and pants outside. Treat clothes with tick spray. Walk on open trails.

Check clothes and pets for ticks before coming inside.

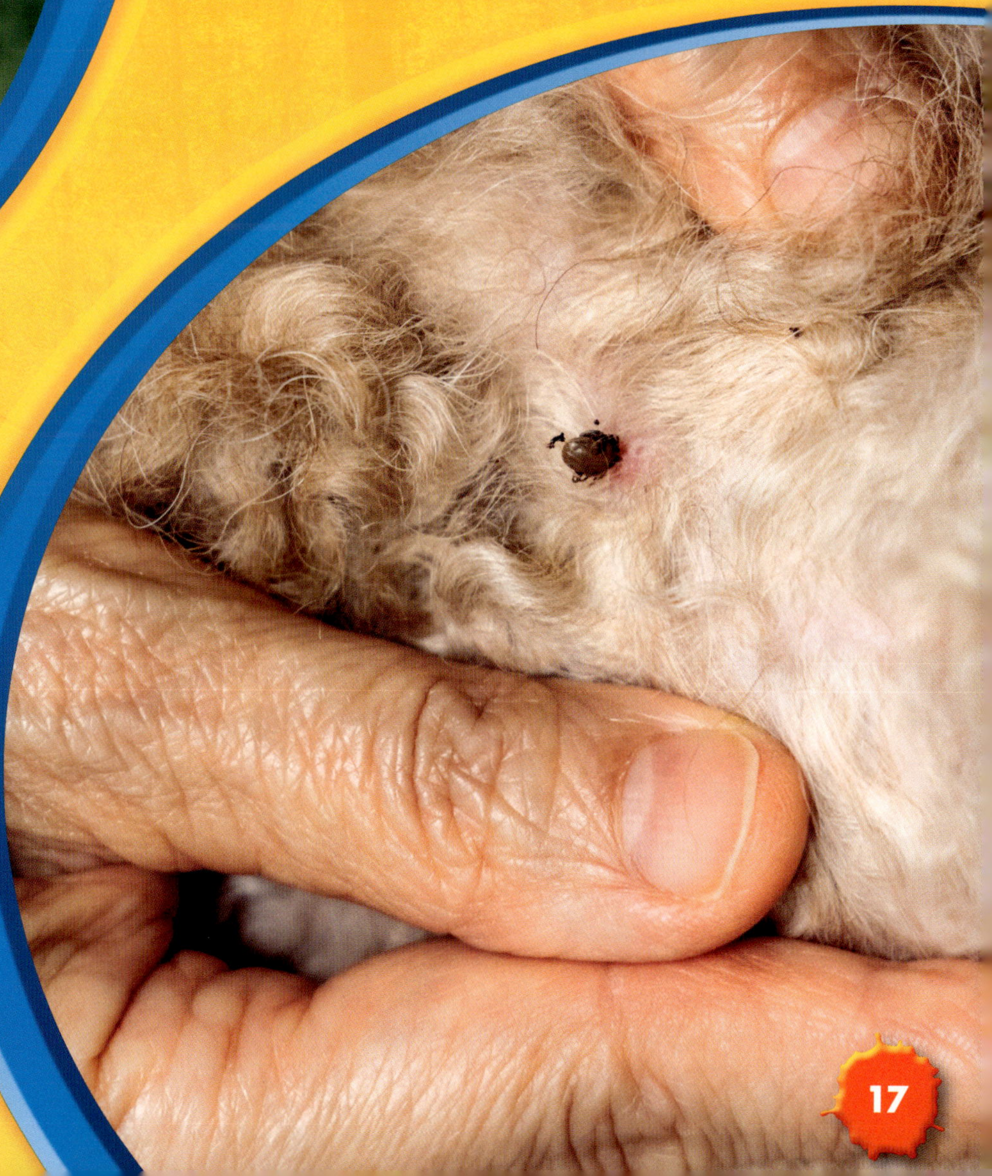

Ticks like warm places on the body. Check under arms and behind knees. Check the head and inside the ears.

Healing Hero

Name

Doctor Willy Burgdorfer

Year Helped

1982

How He Helped

Found the bacterium that causes Lyme disease

Remove any attached ticks with tweezers.

Lyme disease is treated with **antibiotics**. They need to be taken for at least 14 days.

If it is not treated quickly, Lyme disease can lead to problems years later. Check for ticks!

taking antibiotics

Glossary

antibiotics—medicines that treat infections caused by bacteria

attaches—joins something

bacterium—a very tiny life form that can make a person sick

disease—a sickness

fever—a higher-than-normal body temperature

infection—an illness caused by a bacteria or virus

rash—an area of itchy, red spots on the skin

rodents—small animals such as mice, voles, and squirrels

saliva—a watery fluid in the mouth that breaks down food

tick—a bug that attaches to skin and sucks blood; deer ticks often spread Lyme disease.

To Learn More

AT THE LIBRARY

Klepeis, Alicia Z. *Antibiotics*. Minneapolis, Minn.: Jump!, 2021.

Mould, Steve. *The Bacteria Book*. New York, N.Y.: DK Publishing, 2024.

Pettiford, Rebecca. *Malaria*. Minneapolis, Minn.: Bellwether Media, 2027.

ON THE WEB

FACTSURFER

Factsurfer.com gives you a safe, fun way to find more information.

1. Go to www.factsurfer.com.

2. Enter "Lyme disease" into the search box and click 🔍.

3. Select your book cover to see a list of related content.

Index

The images in this book are reproduced through the courtesy of: nechaevkon, front cover (hero), p. 3 (hero); Alexey Androsov, front cover (Splatter left), p. 4; Evgeniyqw, front cover (splatter right); Smileus, front cover (back); Jay Ondreicka, p. 5; Szasz-Fabian Jozsef, p. 5 (inset); Ingo Bartussek, p. 6; AnaKopa, pp. 8, 15 (step 3); Wangkun Jia, p. 9; F1online digitale Bildagentur GmbH/ Alamy Stock Photo, pp. 10-11; KPixMining, pp. 12, 13, 14-15, 15 (step 2), 16, 20-21; artfotoxyz, p. 14; Robert Benson, p. 15 (step 1); Crisp0022, p. 16 (inset); ThamKC, p. 17; Molishka, p. 18; MakroBetz, p. 18 (inset); NIH History Office/ Wikipedia, p. 19; WESTOCK PRODUCTIONS, p. 20.